rspb **Nature Guide**

BIRDS

CATHERINE BRERETON

Illustrated by
KATE M^cLELLAND

BLOOMSBURY

For Liz and Lucy, my birdwatching buddies,
and for Tyra, who has all this to discover — C. B.

For Dad, thank you for all the
lovely walks — love Kate x

BLOOMSBURY CHILDREN'S BOOKS
Bloomsbury Publishing Plc
50 Bedford Square, London, WC1B 3DP, UK

BLOOMSBURY, BLOOMSBURY CHILDREN'S BOOKS and the Diana logo
are trademarks of Bloomsbury Publishing Plc

First published in Great Britain 2020 by Bloomsbury Publishing Plc

Published under licence from RSPB Sales Limited to raise awareness of the RSPB
(charity registration in England and Wales no 207076 and Scotland no SC037654).

For all licensed products sold by Bloomsbury Publishing Limited, Bloomsbury Publishing Limited
will donate a minimum of 2% from all sales to RSPB Sales Ltd, which gives all its distributable
profits through Gift Aid to the RSPB.

A catalogue record for this book is available from the British Library

ISBN: PB: 978-1-5266-0281-7;
eBook: 978-1-5266-1330-1

2 4 6 8 10 9 7 5 3 1

Text by Catherine Brereton

Printed and bound in China by Leo Paper Products, Heshan, Guangdong

FSC
MIX
Paper
FSC® C020056

All papers used by Bloomsbury Publishing Plc are natural, recyclable
product from wood grown in well managed forests and other sources.

To find out more about our authors and books visit
www.bloomsbury.com and sign up for our newsletters

CONTENTS

BIRDS ARE EVERYWHERE!

You can probably see some from your window right now, whether you live in a big city, a town or in the countryside.

You can see birds in your garden, street or local park, or you can take a walk in a nearby wood, beside a river or along a beach. You can watch birds in your favourite local spot every day throughout the year. You can find places near you that are good for spotting birds, and you can visit places especially to see the bird life there.

This book will help you recognise most of the birds you see around you, and find out about how they behave.

Be a birdwatcher

There are lots of ways to enjoy birds. You can watch them on your own, with your friends and family, or join a group of bird fans. You can try to spot as many different birds as you can, or find out all about your favourites. You can draw them, photograph them, help to look after them and much more.

Some people call it birdwatching, some people call it birding – but whatever you call it, prepare to get hooked!

A nature reserve with a lake is a great place for spotting birds.

Birdwatcher's code

• *Be respectful of birds and their home. Remember, the birds' interests come first!*

• *Try to be quiet, patient and still when watching birds. Don't disturb or frighten birds, don't get too close, and keep away from their nests.*

• *Never take birds' eggs (it is against the law) or disturb nests.*

• *Follow the Countryside Code. Ask permission before you go on to private land, and don't walk on farm crops. Make sure you shut gates behind you.*

• *Protect habitats. Don't drop litter, or pick or damage any plants.*

HABITATS

A place where a bird lives is called its habitat. The right habitat will provide the right types of food and places to shelter and nest. Some birds can live in lots of habitats, while others can only live in certain habitats.

Gardens and parks

Gardens and parks are great places for birds to find food and water and somewhere to shelter and to nest. Trees, bushes and other plants provide food and attract insects for birds to eat. Nesting places include trees, sheds, roofs and nest boxes!

Find out how to encourage birds to come to your garden on page 116.

Towns and cities

Some birds are happy living in the middle of towns and cities – in squares and car parks, under bridges and on roofs and ledges. They nest in buildings as well as in trees and bushes, making the most of every scrap of green space they can find.

Fields and hedges

Many wild birds live on farmland. They eat the weeds, insects and small animals that are found in fields, as well as leftover crops. Farms often have hedges, which contain lots of plants that birds like, and are brilliant places for them to nest, shelter and hide.

Woods

Woodlands are some of the richest bird habitats in Britain. Just one tree can support thousands of insects and make thousands of seeds, so it's no surprise that woods are good places for birds. With so many places to hide, it can be tricky to see birds in woodland, but listen out for calls and songs.

Rivers and lakes

All living things need water, and where there's a lot of water there are lots of birds! Some eat the many insects, fish and other small animals that are found in or near rivers and lakes. Some make their nests on islands and in vegetation at the waterside. Some swim on the water, some dive down underneath it, and some just live next to it.

The seaside

Some birds live at sea, nest on cliffs and feed on fish and other sea creatures. Others are found on beaches or estuaries, which are the flat, muddy areas where rivers meet the sea. These places are rich habitats where birds can find food such as insects and shellfish. Birds come and go as the tide goes in and out.

Mountains and moorland

Some birds only live high above most farms and towns. The landscape may be huge stretches of heather moorland or conifer woodland with mountain streams. Many moorland birds are small and well camouflaged, so they are difficult to spot.

BIRDWATCHING THROUGH THE YEAR

Birdwatching never stays the same. It changes with the seasons – there are different birds to see, and the birds you see every day are doing different things. There's always something fun to watch!

In spring

- Look out for birds starting to make their nests.

- Watch for your first swallow.

- See baby birds as they hatch – waterbirds such as ducks, geese and swans are some of the easiest to observe.

- Why not get up early to hear the dawn chorus? This is when lots of different birds sing their songs very early in the morning, about an hour before it gets light. Robins, blackbirds and thrushes start the singing, then many other small birds join in.

In summer

- Get to know the young birds in your local spot. How many are there? How do they look different from the adults?

- Why not go on a boat trip to visit a seabird colony – it will be crowded, noisy and smelly but you will see some amazing birds!

On holiday
If you visit somewhere on holiday, have fun getting to know the birds that live there. Books or websites will tell you about the local birds and other wildlife.

In autumn

- Look out for swallows and house martins gathering, ready to head south for the winter.

- Clean your bird feeders and fill them up (remember, you can feed birds all year round).

- Watch for jays burying acorns.

Why not keep a bird diary, noting down every bird you see, and when and where you saw it? If you do the same year after year you can build up an idea of how the timings change or stay the same.

Migration

Many birds migrate, spending the summer in one part of the world, laying eggs and raising their chicks there, and flying to another part of the world for the winter.

In winter

- Keep topping up your bird feeders and enjoy watching the birds that come to eat.

- In freezing weather, make sure you put out water for birds to drink, as most water will be turned to ice.

- Look for flocks of fieldfares and redwings.

- Listen out for the few birds that sing in the winter, e.g. robin, song thrush, mistle thrush and great tit.

- Visit a wetland nature reserve where you'll see winter visitors — waders, ducks, geese and swans.

RSPB Big Garden Birdwatch UK

Every January, millions of people join in the Big Garden Birdwatch UK, counting the different birds they see in their gardens and telling the RSPB what they've seen. Find out more at rspb.org.uk/birdwatch.

What do birds do all year?

Each type of bird has its own busy schedule throughout the year. Keep watching as the year unfolds and you'll see them doing different things.

Robin

In **spring**, a male robin sings its loud, pretty song to attract a mate. The female makes a nest out of dried leaves and moss, lined with hair and feathers. She lays five to six eggs and sits on them for about 13 days. When the chicks hatch, both parents are busy feeding them for about 14 days until they leave the nest.

In **summer**, the spotty brown chicks hop around learning to feed. The parents might have another brood of chicks.

In **winter** and **spring**, robins quarrel with other robins to defend their territory. They sing a slower, sad-sounding song.

Blackbird

In **spring**, blackbirds sing from a high perch. They start very early in the morning. Male birds chase each other noisily and show off to females by running about with their tails fanned and wings drooped. The females build the nest. They lay three to five eggs and sit on them for about 14 days. When the chicks hatch, both parents feed them worms and caterpillars. The chicks leave the nest and hop about for a few days before they learn to fly.

In **autumn** and **winter**, when there are not so many worms about, blackbirds eat berries. They can cope with cold weather quite well.

All year, you can see blackbirds standing and tilting their heads towards the ground, looking out for worms moving under the surface.

Blue tit

In **spring**, blue tits find a nest. You might see blue tits 'courtship feeding'. This is when a male catches food for a female, so she can eat enough to have the energy to produce her eggs. Juicy caterpillars are their favourite. Then the female lays 7 to 14 eggs and sits on them for about 14 days. When the chicks hatch, the parents may catch hundreds of caterpillars a day to feed them!

In **summer**, chicks leave the nest. You may see groups of young blue tits with yellow faces.

In **winter**, blue tits fly from garden to garden looking for food. They quarrel with other birds at the bird table — they may steal food from great tits, and great tits may steal theirs!

Swallow

In **spring**, our swallows are travelling up western Africa. They arrive in the UK from April onwards.

In **summer**, swallows build nests out of mud and straw, lay eggs and feed their chicks. Watch swallows busily flying back and forth to the nest hundreds of times a day. They may have two broods in a summer.

Winter at the lake
Winter is a good time to see waterbirds on lakes and ponds. Some ducks, geese and swans arrive to spend the winter here.

In **autumn**, large groups of swallows gather ready to set off on their migration. Some of the chicks are only a few weeks old when they fly off on their long journey.

In **winter**, our swallows are in South Africa, feeding on insects there.

WHAT TO LOOK OUT FOR

To identify a bird, you need to look out for clues that tell you what it is and tell it apart from other birds. First of all, look at its size. Can you compare it to a bird you know well, such as a duck, pigeon or sparrow perhaps? Then look at its shape. Does it have a round body or a long body? What shape is its tail? What shape is its beak? How about its legs? Here are some examples of well known birds and their shapes.

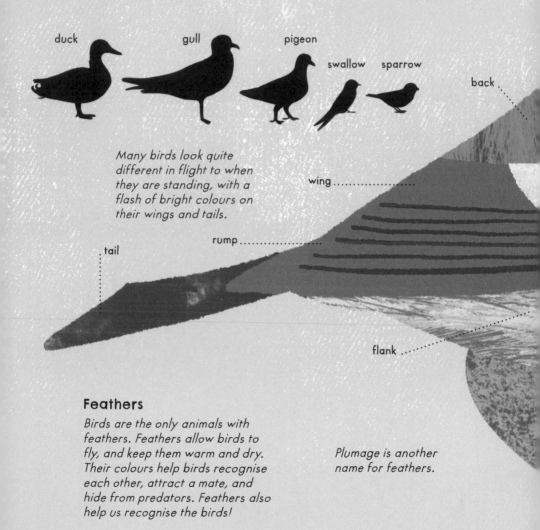

duck

gull

pigeon

swallow

sparrow

back

Many birds look quite different in flight to when they are standing, with a flash of bright colours on their wings and tails.

wing

rump

tail

flank

Feathers

Birds are the only animals with feathers. Feathers allow birds to fly, and keep them warm and dry. Their colours help birds recognise each other, attract a mate, and hide from predators. Feathers also help us recognise the birds!

Plumage is another name for feathers.

crown

nape

forehead

Beak and **bill** are different words for the same thing.

chin

throat

breast

belly

leg

Moulting

Feathers get damaged and worn out easily. Birds lose old feathers and grow new ones. This is called moulting. Birds usually grow bright new feathers in spring and some may have duller-coloured feathers at other times of year.

Mallard ducks are a good example of this. There is a special name for the dull brown feathers male ducks grow – it's called 'eclipse plumage'. In late summer it looks like all the males have disappeared – but they grow their bright feathers again in autumn.

13

Behaviour

You can tell a lot about birds by how they behave. How do they fly? Fast or slow, hovering or fluttering, straight or up-and-down? On the ground, do they hop, walk or run? Are they on their own or in pairs or flocks? Noisy or shy? What are they eating, and how? All these observations will help you identify a bird and learn more about it.

Birds and the environment

Birds live everywhere, but they and the places where they live need to be kept safe. There are lots of nature reserves where birds and their habitats are protected (for more information, see page 123). But we all need to do our bit to look after the whole environment, for birds, other wildlife, and people too.

Song

Calls and songs are a great way of telling birds apart. Why not learn some of the easier calls and listen out for them next time you go birdwatching? The RSPB website has sound clips for all the birds in this book.

HOW TO USE THIS BOOK

The main section of this book, pages 16–115, is a **nature guide**. It will help you to name many of the birds that you might see in the UK and Ireland.

Fact box

For many of the birds in the nature guide you will find handy information in a fact box. Here is the key:

- tells you the length of an adult bird – this is measured from the tip of its beak to the tip of its tail
- tells you whether the bird is here all year round or visits in summer or winter only
- tells you that this bird is common
- tells you where the bird lives (its habitat)
- describes the bird's call or song
- tells you what the bird eats

Pictures

The pictures show each bird's shape, colour and markings and how it perches or flies. They show you if the male and female look different from each other.

pied wagtail (female)

pied wagtail (male)

Descriptions

The descriptions tell you what each bird looks like and give information about its behaviour.

Little grebe

The little grebe is a small, round waterbird with a brown body, chestnut neck and cheeks and a fluffy bottom. It lives in lakes and rivers, where it swims busily, searching for fish or insects to eat. It is shy and secretive, and dives under water or hides among water plants when something frightens it.

The little grebe is one of the smallest swimming birds in the UK.

little grebe

Sometimes a little grebe jumps with a splash before it dives.

little grebe

🐦 25–29 cm

🦗 year-round

👀 common

🏠 lakes, rivers, canals

🔊 loud, high-pitched trill

🌿 insects and their larvae, water snails, small fish

Stripy chicks ride on their parents' backs to stay safe.

great crested grebe chick

Great crested grebes build floating nests out of reeds.

Great crested grebe

The great crested grebe is an elegant bird with a long white neck. In summer, it grows bright feathers on the sides of its head, which it uses in an elaborate dance to attract a mate. The grebes shake their heads to show off their crests, fluff up their feathers, and dive for waterweed to give to each other.

great crested grebe

great crested grebe

🐦 46–51 cm

🦐 year-round

🔭 common

🏠 lakes

🎵 mostly silent

🌿 mainly fish, also insect larvae, amphibians

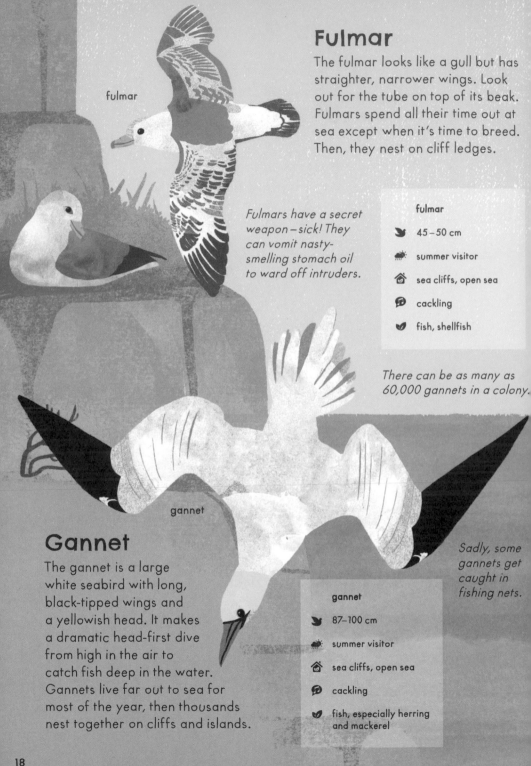

fulmar

Fulmar

The fulmar looks like a gull but has straighter, narrower wings. Look out for the tube on top of its beak. Fulmars spend all their time out at sea except when it's time to breed. Then, they nest on cliff ledges.

Fulmars have a secret weapon—sick! They can vomit nasty-smelling stomach oil to ward off intruders.

fulmar

🕊 45–50 cm

☀ summer visitor

🏠 sea cliffs, open sea

🗣 cackling

🌿 fish, shellfish

There can be as many as 60,000 gannets in a colony.

gannet

Gannet

The gannet is a large white seabird with long, black-tipped wings and a yellowish head. It makes a dramatic head-first dive from high in the air to catch fish deep in the water. Gannets live far out to sea for most of the year, then thousands nest together on cliffs and islands.

Sadly, some gannets get caught in fishing nets.

gannet

🕊 87–100 cm

☀ summer visitor

🏠 sea cliffs, open sea

🗣 cackling

🌿 fish, especially herring and mackerel

Cormorant

The cormorant is a large waterbird with a long neck, hooked beak and dark body. Cormorants are expert fishers — they swim along the water and then dive to catch their prey. They like to sit with their wings stretched out.

Shag

The shag is similar to the cormorant, but it has a thinner beak, darker body and no white face. It has iridescent (shiny) green feathers, but these usually look black. It is also an expert diver.

cormorant

- 80–100 cm
- year-round
- sea, lakes, rivers
- croaks and growls
- fish

cormorant

shag

Cormorants probably sit like this to dry off their feathers after fishing.

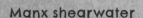

Manx shearwater

The Manx shearwater spends all day feeding at sea. It is black on top and white underneath. It flies with stiff wings and skims or 'shears' the surface of the water.

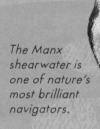

The Manx shearwater is one of nature's most brilliant navigators.

Eider

The eider is a sea duck. The male is black and white, with green markings on its head. The female is brown. Eiders have strong beaks that they use to grab and crush shellfish.

Storm petrel

The storm petrel is a tiny seabird, the size of a sparrow. It is black with a white bottom and white stripes under its wings. It flutters along behind ships, with its feet touching the water.

Eiders line their nests with very soft 'down' feathers. We use eiderdown to make bed covers to keep us warm, too.

Great skua
The great skua is the pirate of the bird world! It is a large, powerful bird like a giant brown gull. It attacks other seabirds and steals their food, and kills and eats their chicks, too.

Red-throated diver
Out at sea in winter you may see a bird that swims like a duck but is a different shape. This is a diver. The red-throated diver is greyish with a red throat.

Divers can swim fast under water and can chase fish.

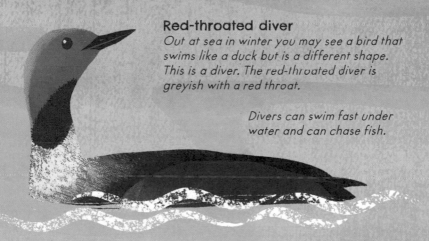

Grey heron

The grey heron is a very large bird
with long legs, a long neck and a
sharp, dagger-like beak. It has a grey
back and a white head with a black stripe.
An expert at catching fish, the heron stands
very still, patiently watching the water, then
quickly strikes. It stabs its prey and
swallows it whole.

grey heron

grey heron

🕊 90 –98 cm

🦟 year-round

🔭 common

🏠 lakes, rivers, marshes,
estuaries

🔊 deep croak

🍃 mainly fish, also frogs
and small mammals

*Grey herons
use their toe
like a comb
to brush their
feathers.*

Little egret

The little egret is a small white heron with black legs and yellow feet.

Bittern

The bittern is a rare, very secretive bird. It nests in reedbeds. Its stripy markings keep it well camouflaged among the reeds. The male bittern has a loud, booming call that can be heard up to five kilometres away.

Mute swan

The mute swan is a large, graceful waterbird. It is white apart from a bright orange bill with a black bump on top. It has a long, S-shaped neck that it uses to reach deep into the water to feed on plants. Swans make big nests of grass and reeds near the water. Cygnets sometimes ride on their parents' backs to keep warm and stay safe from predators.

A male swan is called a cob and a female is called a pen.

mute swan

🕊 125–155 cm

🌧 year-round

👀 common

🏠 lakes, rivers, canals

🗯 loud hiss when angry

🍃 water plants, insects, snails

cygnets

mute swan
(adults)

Mute swan
pairs usually
stay together
for life.

Swans have more
feathers on their
body than any
other bird — about
25,000 altogether.

Canada goose

The Canada goose is a big waterbird originally from Canada – a large number now live in the wild in the UK as a result of birds escaping captivity. It has a long black neck, white cheeks and chin, and a greyish-brown body. You can see flocks of Canada geese in parks – they swim in ponds and lakes and waddle about on grass nearby. They are noisy birds and make a loud honking, trumpeting noise. In their native North America, they migrate long distances, flying in a V pattern, with one goose as the leader and the flock following behind.

Canada goose

🐦 56 – 110 cm

🐝 year-round

👀 common

🏠 lakes, rivers, canals

🔊 loud trumpeting

🌿 roots, grass, leaves, seeds

Canada goose

Like all ducks, geese and swans, Canada geese have webbed feet.

A group of geese in the sky is called a skein, team or flock. On the ground it's a gaggle.

Mallard

The mallard is our most common and familiar duck. It is a dabbling duck, which means it feeds on the surface of the water. Watch as it tips itself tail-up to reach for food. The male, or drake, has a dark green head and yellow beak, and a bright flash of shiny blue on its wing that really stands out when it flies. The female is speckled brown and she has the shiny blue flash, too. Only the female makes the well-known 'quack, quack' call.

	mallard
🐦	50 – 65 cm
🐛	year-round
🔭	common
🏠	ponds, lakes, rivers, canals, marshes
🗨	*quack, quack*
🌿	seeds, plants, insects, shellfish, small fish

Mallards can be found anywhere on or near water, from small ponds or streams to large lakes.

mallard (male)

The female makes a nest of grass, leaves and soft down feathers.

mallard (female)

Mallard ducklings leave the nest within a day of hatching and can swim and feed themselves straight away. But it is a while before they can fly.

duckling

Tufted duck

The tufted duck is easy to spot by the tuft or crest on the back of its head. Males are black and white, females are dark brown and both have yellow eyes. Watch them dive time and time again to catch food. These ducks gather in large flocks in winter.

tufted duck	
🐦	40 – 47 cm
☀️	year-round
👀	common
🏠	lakes, parks
🗣️	mostly silent
🌿	shellfish, insects, water plants

tufted duck
(male)

tufted duck
(female)

Pochard

The pochard is a small, plump diving duck. The male is easy to recognise – look for its rusty-red head and neck and its black breast and tail. You may see pochards sleeping on the water in the daytime, as they often prefer to feed after dark.

pochard	
🐦	42 – 49 cm
☀️	year-round
🏠	lakes, parks
🗣️	mostly silent
🌿	water plants, water snails, small fish, insects

Goldeneye

This duck has bright golden-yellow eyes, as its name suggests. Its head looks like it's been puffed up. The male goldeneye is black and white, with a green-black head and a white spot on its face. The female has a chocolate-brown head.

goldeneye

- 42–50 cm
- winter visitor – a few nest in Scotland
- lakes and rivers in forests
- mainly silent, but male sometimes makes a loud *zeee-zeee* call and a low growling
- shellfish, small fish, insects, water plants

A goldeneye can stay under water for up to a minute.

goldeneye (female)

goldeneye (male)

pochard (female)

The pochard makes an obvious jump before it dives.

pochard (male)

Greylag goose

The greylag goose is a large goose. It is greyish-brown with an orange bill and pink legs. These geese gather in large flocks and often mix with Canada geese. White farmyard geese are descended from greylag geese.

Brent goose

The Brent goose is a small goose, the size of a mallard. It is a winter visitor around the coasts of Britain. It has a black head and chest and a white pattern on its neck.

Barnacle goose

The barnacle goose is a winter visitor. It is smaller and greyer than the Canada goose, and the whole of its face is white. Its call sounds like a dog yapping. It nests on islands in the Arctic. The goslings have to make dangerous jumps from their nests into the water.

Shelduck

The shelduck is a big white duck with a dark green head and neck, chestnut belly and a red beak. The male has a bump on its beak, the female does not. Shelducks love to eat tiny water snails.

Shoveler

The shoveler has a green head like a mallard, but look for its large, shovel-shaped bill. Inside this bill is a special sieve for filtering food from the surface of the water.

Teal

The teal is a small, shy duck. The male has a chestnut head with a green flash, and a green band on its wing.

A male teal never visits the nest, as he is so brightly coloured he would make it too easy for predators to spot the nest.

Whooper swan

The whooper swan is a winter visitor from Iceland. It has a pointed yellow patch on its beak. It makes a honking noise like an old-fashioned car horn.

Bewick's swan

The Bewick's swan flies over from Siberia each winter. It has a round yellow patch on its beak. It is the smallest of Britain's three types of swan.

red kite

🐦 60 – 66 cm

🐛 year-round

🏠 farmland, woodland

🎵 high-pitched *pee-ooo-eee*

🍃 mainly carrion, also worms, small mammals, birds

Red kites twist their forked tale in flight. This helps them to steer.

red kite

Red kite

The red kite is a large bird of prey with a pale head, reddish-brown body and reddish-orange, forked tail. Like all birds of prey, it has a hooked beak and sharp claws called talons. It was once very rare in the UK, but a conservation project has saved it from extinction.

buzzard

- 🐦 51–57 cm
- 🌧 year-round
- 👓 common
- 🏠 hilly areas, farmland, woodland
- 💬 high-pitched *pee-uuu*
- 🌿 rabbits, voles, birds, carrion, insects, worms

sparrowhawk

- 🐦 28–38 cm
- 🌧 year-round
- 👓 common
- 🏠 forests, farmland, towns and cities
- 💬 chattering *kew-kew-kew* when nesting
- 🌿 small birds

A buzzard can fly for a long time without flapping its wings.

buzzard

Buzzard

The buzzard is a large bird of prey. It is brownish all over, with broad wings. Like all birds of prey it has excellent eyesight. Look for it soaring high in the sky watching for small animals on the ground, or perched on a fence post or telegraph pole. Rabbits are its favourite food.

sparrowhawk (male)

Sparrowhawk

The sparrowhawk is a small bird of prey. Its white 'eyebrows' give it a fierce expression. It has a barred pattern across its front – the male has a grey back and the female has a brown back. The female is also much bigger in size than the male. Sparrowhawks fly very fast. They chase and catch small birds in flight.

Kestrel

The kestrel is a bird of prey with a long tail and pointed wings. It hovers in the air. You might see one hovering by the roadside. It looks completely still except for its quivering wings, then it will dive fast to catch a vole.

kestrel

kestrel

🕊 32–35 cm

🐝 year-round

👓 common

🏠 open areas with rough grassland, towns and cities

🗣 shrill *ki-ki-ki-ki-ki*

🍃 voles, other small mammals, large insects

Hobby

The hobby is a small bird of prey, about the size of a kestrel. It is a fast, agile and graceful flier. It catches insects and small birds in flight – dragonflies are its favourite prey.

peregrine
falcon

A peregrine falcon can dive at about an amazing 240 kph.

Peregrine falcon

The peregrine falcon is a medium-sized bird of prey. Look for its black head and 'moustache' and white cheeks. Peregrine falcons are brilliant hunters and hold the record for being the fastest birds in the world. When one dives, it swoops downwards and knocks its prey out or catches it in mid-air.

peregrine falcon

🐦 36 – 48 cm

🐝 year-round

🏠 hilly areas, towns and cities

📢 harsh, cackling *kek-rek-rek* when nesting

🍃 birds

37

Golden eagle

The golden eagle is a very large bird of prey, much bigger than a buzzard. It is dark brown with a golden head and neck, great, broad wings and a large, powerful hooked beak. It is a rare but impressive sight soaring high over hillsides in parts of Scotland. Golden eagles can catch quite big animals, even foxes, but mostly eat hares, grouse and carrion.

golden eagle	
🦅	75 – 88 cm
☀️	year-round
🏠	moorlands, high mountains, remote islands
🔊	usually silent
🌿	mammals, birds, carrion

An eagle hunts by flying low and then pouncing.

golden eagle

After a big meal, it may not need to eat for several days.

An eagle's nest is called an eyrie.

A golden eagle
can live for
over 30 years.

osprey

It can close its nostrils to stop water getting up its nose when it dives.

An osprey has spines under its toes to help catch its slippery prey.

Osprey

The osprey is a large bird of prey that hunts fish. It has a dark streak across its eye that looks like a mask. To catch its prey it makes a spectacular dive. It plunges head first towards the water, then, at the last moment, sticks its feet out and grabs a fish. Ospreys make their nests in pine trees. The male osprey brings a fish to the female, who tears off pieces to feed to the young.

osprey

55 – 58 cm

summer visitor

lakes, large rivers, estuaries

usually silent

fish

Pairs return to the same nest year after year.

The nest is built of sticks and lined with moss, bark and grass.

Red grouse

The red grouse is a plump game bird that lives on heather moors. The male is reddish-brown with a red wattle over each eye. The female is a duller brown and doesn't have the red over the eye. Both are well camouflaged for hiding in the heather.

red grouse
(male)

red grouse	
	37 – 42 cm
	year-round
	heather moorland
	call sounds like 'go back, go back!'
	heather, seeds, berries, insects

Pheasant

The pheasant is a large game bird originally from Asia. The male has a dark green head, red wattle, brown body and long tail. Some have a white neck ring too. The female is paler. In the countryside you can see pheasants walking at the edges of woods and along hedgerows. You can sometimes get quite close to one before it flies up with a noisy clatter of wings and a loud croak.

pheasant
(male)

pheasant	
	53 – 89 cm
	year-round
	common
	farmland, woodland
	raucous *ko-kok*
	grain, seeds, fruit, insects

Grey partridge

The grey partridge is a shy game bird. The male is grey and brown with an orange face, and the female is a duller brown. Partridges are very well camouflaged and can look like large stones. When danger is near they will often keep still, and only at the last moment will they fly away.

A grey partridge lays one of the largest clutches of eggs in the world for a bird – sometimes as many as 25!

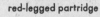

grey partridge (male)

grey partridge

🐦 29 – 31 cm

🐛 year-round

🏠 farmland

🗣 grating *kerrick* call

🌿 seeds, leaves, insects

Red-legged partridge

The red-legged partridge is a little larger than the grey partridge and originally from France. It has white cheeks, a red bill, black patterns on its face and colourful markings on its breast and flank. Although it's brightly coloured, it's still well camouflaged.

Red-legged partridges often run rather than fly away from danger.

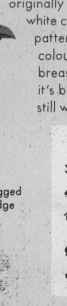

red-legged partridge (male)

red-legged partridge

🐦 32 – 34 cm

🐛 year-round

🏠 farmland and open woodland

🗣 loud *chuck-chukka-chuck*

🌿 seeds, leaves, roots

Moorhen

The moorhen is a waterbird. It is nearly all black, with a red and yellow beak, white on its side and under its tail, and long, green legs and toes. Moorhens live on ponds, rivers and lakes. Watch them bob their heads back and forwards when they swim and also when they walk.

moorhen

🕊 32–35 cm

🐛 year-round

🔭 common

🏠 lakes, ponds, ditches, rivers

🔊 loud *kruuuk*

🌿 water plants, berries, worms, snails, spiders, insects, small fish, eggs

moorhen

Their long, thin toes are good for climbing.

Moorhen chicks are black and fluffy.

Coot

The coot is a waterbird. It is easy to get it mixed up with a moorhen, and you will often see them in the same places. The coot is bigger, and all black except for its white beak and forehead. Coots are quarrelsome and often fight each other. You will see them diving underwater a lot.

	coot
🕊	36–38 cm
✴	year-round
🔭	common
⌂	lakes, ponds
🔊	loud *kowk*
🍃	algae, water plants, shellfish, snails, insects

A coot's white forehead looks a bit like a bald head, giving rise to the expression 'as bald as a coot'.

A coot has flaps of skin between its lobed toes to help it swim.

coot

Oystercatcher

The oystercatcher is a big black-and-white wader with a bright orange bill. It is noisy and easy to spot. An oystercatcher's strong beak is great for catching shellfish. The bird sticks its beak into the sand to find a shell, then pulls the shell open or bashes it until it breaks.

oystercatcher

oystercatcher

🐦 40 – 45 cm

☀ year-round

👀 common

🏠 coasts, estuaries, lakes, rivers

🗣 loud, high-pitched *peep peep peep*

🌿 mussels, other shellfish, crabs, worms

Look out for gulls and crows stealing food from oystercatchers!

Avocet

The avocet is another black-and-white wader.
It has a slender, turned-up bill. Avocets feed
in shallow water at estuaries and lagoons.
They sweep their bills from side to side, filtering
out tiny shrimps or larvae, or snap up small
creatures from the water. They have long
legs for wading (which means walking in
water or mud).

avocet

*The avocet is the
symbol of the RSPB.*

avocet

🦅 40 – 45 cm

🌦 year-round

🏠 coasts, estuaries

🔊 *klute klute* call when alarmed

🌿 shrimps, insect larvae,
insects, worms

Lapwing

The lapwing is a colourful, noisy farmland bird, the size of a dove. From a distance it looks black and white, but close up you can see it has a black cap and crest and an iridescent green back. The male is quite an acrobat in flight – it climbs and then tumbles again and again to impress its mate. Listen for the *peewit* call and look out for large flocks of lapwings in farm fields.

The lapwing is sometimes called other names: peewit and green plover.

lapwing

- 28 – 31 cm
- year-round
- common
- farmland, marshland
- *peewit*
- worms, beetles, flies, ants, snails

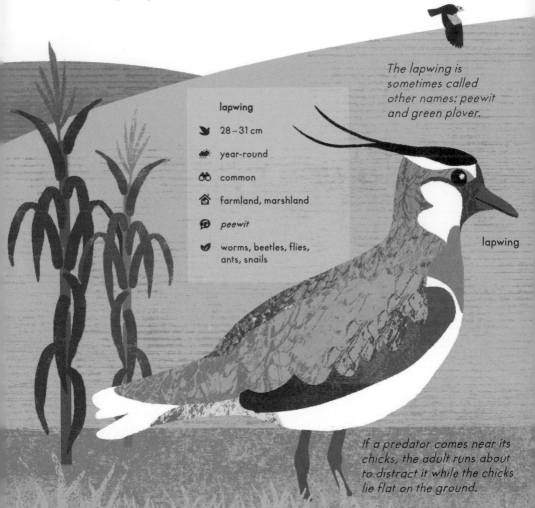

lapwing

If a predator comes near its chicks, the adult runs about to distract it while the chicks lie flat on the ground.

Woodcock

The woodcock is a plump, brown bird with a very long, straight bill. The tip of its bill is very sensitive and allows it to feel worms wriggling in the soil. It lives in woodland, where it is very well camouflaged among fallen leaves. It is secretive and is mainly active at dusk.

woodcock

🐦 33 – 35 cm

🌦 year-round

🏠 woodland, moorland

🎵 *croak*

🌿 worms, beetles, spiders, caterpillars, snails

woodcock

Curlew

The curlew is Britain's largest wader. It has streaky brown feathers and a very long, curved beak. It wades in deep water but it's often seen on grassland or moorland. It uses its long beak to poke for food such as crabs and shellfish in mud or under water. It gets its name from its call, which sounds like 'cur-lew'.

curlew

curlew

🐦 50 – 60 cm

🦟 year-round

🏠 moorland, coasts, estuaries

🗣 *cur-lew*

🍃 crabs, shellfish, snails, worms, insects

Greenshank
The greenshank is a medium-sized wader, rarer and slightly bigger than a redshank. It has greenish-grey legs and a long, very slightly upturned bill. It nests in wild, remote places.

redshank

Redshank

The redshank is a medium-sized wader with a long red beak and red legs. It is a noisy bird and is constantly on the lookout for danger. It has a loud alarm call that warns other birds when trouble is near. When it flies, look for the big white stripes on its wings.

redshank

🐦 27–29 cm

🌧 year-round

🏠 estuaries, marshes, moorland

📣 ringing *teeu-tu-tu* alarm call

🍃 shrimps, small fish, crabs, shellfish, snails, worms, flies

Grey plover

The grey plover is a winter visitor. In winter it is grey and white, with black 'armpits' visible in flight. It has a thin, straight beak and picks up food from the surface of the mud.

Ringed plover

The ringed plover has a black 'mask' and a black ring around its chest. It has a short, orange beak. It runs along, stops, bobs down to pick up food then runs along again.

Knot

The knot is mainly a winter visitor to Britain. It gathers in flocks of thousands of birds, and they look like clouds of smoke when they fly.

Turnstone

The turnstone is a small, busy wader with a reddish-brown back and a black-and-white head and chest. It uses its short, thick beak to turn over stones to find food underneath. This is how it gets its name.

Common sandpiper

The common sandpiper is a small wader. It has a thin, dark beak. It bobs its head up and down all the time and wags its tail as it runs along the shore. It can be seen along rivers too.

Snipe

The snipe is a secretive wader with a very long, straight bill. The bill is sensitive and flexible. The snipe pokes it into the ground and can feel worms moving about, then it catches the worms in the end of its bill. Snipes make a bleating sound called drumming in spring as they dive through the air.

Black-headed gull

The black-headed gull is a smallish gull. Its name is a bit misleading because its head is chocolate-brown rather than black, and in winter it turns white with a black smudge. These gulls are common at the coast and inland, on farmland and at rubbish tips. You'll see them on playing fields too. They are noisy and gather in large flocks. They eat almost anything.

black-headed gull

🐦 34–37 cm

☀️ year-round

👓 common

🏠 coasts, rivers, fields, rubbish tips

🔊 harsh *keeyar* call

🍃 worms, insects, spiders, slugs, crabs, small fish, carrion, scraps of humans' food

black-headed gull

Common gull
The common gull has a yellow beak and legs. It looks like a smaller version of the herring gull.

Herring gull

The herring gull is white, with a grey back and wings, pink legs and a yellow beak with a red spot. Its loud wailing cry is the sound of the seaside, but it is found almost everywhere, not just at the coast. These large gulls are great parents and very clever. They make the most of every opportunity to get food. Watch out for your ice-cream or fish and chips!

herring gull

🐦 55–67 cm

🐛 year-round

🔭 common

🏠 seaside, rivers, towns and cities

💬 various loud mewing and wailing cries

🍃 carrion, seeds, fruit, insects, fish, eggs, young birds, small mammals, scraps of humans' food

herring gull

herring gull (young)

Look out for the herring gull's pink legs – a way to tell it apart from other gulls.

Common tern

Terns look like gulls but are lighter and more delicate. The common tern has a black head, a red beak with a black tip and a long, forked tail. It is very graceful in flight and is sometimes called a 'sea swallow'. It hovers over the water before diving to catch fish.

common tern

common tern

🐦 31–35 cm

☀️ summer visitor

🏠 seaside

🔊 high-pitched *keee-yaaarr*

🌿 fish

Arctic tern

Arctic tern

🐦 33–35 cm

☀️ summer visitor

🏠 seaside

🔊 like common tern, but higher pitched

🌿 fish

Arctic tern

The Arctic tern has a black head, red beak and a long, forked tail. It is difficult to tell common and Arctic terns apart — their beaks are different but this may be hard to see. The Arctic tern makes one of the longest migrations of any animal: a round trip of nearly 40,000 km from the Arctic to Antarctica and back.

Sandwich tern

The Sandwich tern has a black head with a frilly black crest, a black bill with a yellow tip, and black legs. It is the biggest and palest of our terns. Sandwich terns nest on sandy and stony beaches. Many of their nests only survive because they are on nature reserves.

Sandwich tern

- 🕊 36–41 cm
- ☀ summer visitor
- ⌂ seaside
- 🗣 harsh *ki-rrric*
- 🍃 fish

Sandwich tern

Take care to stay away from tern colonies so as not to disturb them.

little tern

- 🕊 22–24 cm
- ☀ summer visitor
- 🔭 seaside
- 🗣 shrill *krik-krik*
- 🍃 fish

Little tern

little tern

The little tern has a black cap with a white forehead, and a yellow bill. It is a small seabird that makes a chattering noise. Its eggs are very well camouflaged on pebbly beaches, which is good for protection from predators but dangerous when clumsy-footed humans are walking about.

Kittiwake

The kittiwake is a medium-sized gull. It is white with a grey back, yellow beak and black feet. It really is a 'sea' gull as it is the only one of our gulls that finds food solely in the sea. It nests in large, noisy colonies on cliffs. Its name comes from its call — a noisy 'kitteewa-aaake'.

kittiwake

kittiwake

38–40 cm

year-round

sea cliffs, open sea

kitteewa-aaake call

fish, other sea creatures

Razorbill

The razorbill is a medium-sized seabird. It is dark chocolate-brown on its head and back, and white underneath. It has a thick, flat bill with white stripes on it. It spends the winter out at sea and only comes to land to breed.

razorbill

razorbill

🐦 37–39 cm

☀️ year-round

🏠 sea cliffs, open sea

🗣️ growling calls at nest

🌿 fish

guillemot

Guillemot

The guillemot is a medium-sized seabird, slimmer than a razorbill with a more slender beak. It is dark chocolate-brown and white, and looks a bit like a penguin. Some guillemots have a pattern that looks like spectacles around each eye. They nest in large, noisy colonies like the kittiwake on rocky sea cliffs and lay their eggs on cliff ledges.

guillemot

🐦 38–41 cm

☀️ year-round

🏠 sea cliffs, open sea

🗣️ growling calls at nest

🌿 fish, crabs

Puffin

The puffin is a black-and-white seabird with a colourful red, blue and yellow beak. You can sometimes see a puffin with lots of sand eels in its beak, which is colourful only in summer and turns mostly grey in winter. In fact its beak is great for catching fish and a puffin can even open its beak without the fish falling out, as it has hooks inside the beak that hold them in place. On land it looks funny as it waddles about, but it flies very fast and can swim strongly underwater.

puffin

Puffins usually stay in the same pairs all their life.

A puffin uses its webbed feet as brakes when landing on the ground.

puffin

🐦 26–29 cm

🕷 year-round

🏠 sea cliffs and open sea

📢 growling calls at nest

🌿 fish

Puffins nest in burrows.

Town pigeon

The town pigeon or feral pigeon is usually mainly grey, although it can also be black, white or brown. It often has a green and purple shiny patch on its neck, a white rump and black wing bars. These pigeons are found almost everywhere and gather in large flocks in towns and cities. They are very tame.

town pigeon

town pigeon	
🕊	31–34 cm
☀	year-round
🔭	common
🏠	towns and cities, cliffs, farmland
🎵	cooing calls
🌿	grain and other seeds, scraps of humans' food

Town pigeons aren't fussy eaters – they will eat scraps of human food as well as grains and seeds.

Town pigeons roost and nest on buildings.

A woodpigeon's wings make a lot of noise when it takes off.

woodpigeon

woodpigeon

🕊 40–42 cm

🐛 year-round

🔭 common

🏠 farmland, woodland, parks, gardens

🎵 five-part call *coo-COO-coo, coo-coo*

🌿 grain, plant buds, leaves and seeds, especially cabbage and peas, beetles and other insects

Woodpigeon

The woodpigeon is our largest and most common pigeon. It is grey with green and white patches on its neck. Look out for white bars on its wings when it flies. The woodpigeon is common on farmland and in woods and towns. Listen out for its call, a soothing 'coo-COO-coo, coo-coo'.

63

turtle dove

Turtle dove
The turtle dove is smaller and darker than a collared dove. It has a scaly pattern on its back, and black-and-white neck stripes. It is a summer visitor and is becoming increasingly rare.

Collared dove

The collared dove is smaller than a woodpigeon. It is pinkish-grey with a black 'collar' on its neck. When it flies you can see white on its tail. Also look out for its red eyes and reddish feet. Collared doves are often seen in pairs in parks, gardens and farms.

collared dove

collared dove

🐦 31–33 cm

🕷 year-round

🏠 farmland, woodland, gardens

🎵 three-part *coo-COO-coo*

🌿 grain, seeds, fruit, sometimes insects

Cuckoo

The cuckoo looks like a small bird of prey. But you are far more likely to hear it than see it. Its famous 'cuc-koo' call is a sign of spring. Cuckoos lay their eggs in other birds' nests. When a cuckoo chick hatches, it pushes all the other eggs or chicks out of its nest, and the host bird looks after the cuckoo chick.

cuckoo

- 32–34 cm
- summer visitor
- moorland, farmland, reed beds, coasts
- loud *cuc-koo* in spring
- caterpillars and other insects

Cuckoos are becoming rarer because of food shortages in the UK and drought in Africa where they spend the winter.

cuckoo

A mother cuckoo may lay as many as 22 eggs in different nests.

Cuckoos like to eat hairy caterpillars — they shake them to get rid of the nasty substances in the hairs before they tuck in.

Barn owl

The barn owl is a mainly white owl. It has a heart-shaped face and is snow-white underneath. It hunts at dusk. Like all owls the barn owl uses its superb hearing to find its prey. It has one ear higher than the other to help pinpoint exactly where a sound is coming from. Listen for its call, a ghostly shriek.

A barn owl usually eats about four small mammals per night.

barn owl

- 🐦 33–35 cm
- 🐛 year-round
- 🏠 farmland, woodland
- 📣 high-pitched shrieks and hissing screams
- 🌿 mainly mice, voles, shrews, also rats, small birds, frogs

A barn owl's feathers are super soft to help it fly silently.

barn owl

Owls can turn their heads right round to look backwards.

Tawny owl

The tawny owl is a brown or greyish owl. It roosts in a tree by day and hunts at night, feeding on small mammals and birds, insects and worms. It can see very well in the dark and has excellent hearing too. It is famous for its 'twit-twoo' hoot – that's the sound of a female ('twit') replying to a male ('twoo').

tawny owl

tawny owl

🐦 37–39 cm

🐝 year-round

🏠 woodland, parks, gardens

🔊 *twit-twoo* hoot

🍃 mainly voles, mice, shrews, also birds, worms, insects

'Tawny' means pale reddish-brown.

Little owl

The little owl is a small owl with a flat head, yellow eyes and white 'eyebrows'. The markings on its face make it look like it's frowning. Its call sounds a bit like a mewing kitten and it mainly eats beetles.

Green woodpecker

The green woodpecker is mainly green with a yellow rump and a red cap. The male in particular has a black outline round its red moustache. It often feeds on the ground, hopping clumsily along to look for ants, which are its favourite food. It has a very long, sticky tongue, which it uses to lick ants up and out of their underground tunnels.

The green woodpecker's call sounds like a loud laugh.

green woodpecker
(female)

green woodpecker
(male)

green woodpecker

- 🐦 31–33 cm
- 🕷 year-round
- 🏠 open woodland, parks
- 🗣 loud, laughing *klu-klu-klu-klu*
- 🍃 mainly ants, also beetles, flies, caterpillars

The green woodpecker's tongue is longer than its head and bill combined. It is wrapped all the way behind its eyes and skull when it's not sticking out.

Great spotted woodpecker

The great spotted woodpecker is black and white with a bright red patch under its tail. The male has a red patch on the back of its head, too. It lives in woods and sometimes comes into gardens to feed. It pecks holes in tree bark and pulls insects out to eat.

Woodpeckers have a spongy beak base and strong neck muscles so they can peck without hurting their head.

great spotted woodpecker (male)

great spotted woodpecker

🐦 22–23 cm

🐛 year-round

🔭 common

🏠 woodland, parks, gardens

🎵 loud *tchik!* call

🌿 insects, nuts

great spotted woodpecker (female)

The great spotted woodpecker is hardly ever seen on the ground.

kingfisher

🐦 16–17 cm

🐞 year-round

🏠 slow-flowing rivers,
lakes, canals

🔊 sharp, high-pitched *zeee*

🌿 small fish, water insects

*Kingfishers lay eggs
in tunnels they make
in the riverbank.*

Kingfisher

The kingfisher is a small bird, just a flash of shiny blue and orange flying alongside a river. It is secretive and moves fast, so despite its bright colours it's hard to see. It will sit still at the water's edge watching for fish, then dive into the water with a plop and catch a fish with its dagger-like bill. Then it bashes the fish against a branch and turns it round to swallow it head first.

Winter is a tough time for kingfishers. If the rivers are frozen they cannot get food. They may move to find open water, so can turn up in all sorts of places.

kingfisher

Water pollution is a serious problem for kingfishers.

Swallows are masters of migration.

swallow

During migration, swallows can fly at an average of 300 km a day. They have to cross the Sahara Desert.

Swallow

The swallow is a summer visitor. It has a red throat and is blue-black above and pale below. It has a forked tail with long streamers. It is one of the fastest and most agile fliers, hunting in mid-air by catching flies in its big, wide mouth. Look out for swallows at the end of summer, gathering together on telephone wires as they get ready to migrate south for winter. They will return to the same nest year after year.

swallow

🐦 17–19 cm

🦋 summer

🔭 common

🏠 farmland, villages, ponds

🐦 *vit-vit* call, long twittering song

🌿 flying insects

Swallows can migrate in the daytime, unlike other small birds, which migrate at night.

Young swallows are ready to make their long journey just weeks after leaving the nest.

swift

Swifts have bristles above their eyes that act like sunglasses.

Swifts may go three years without landing once!

Look out for swifts in summer, but by August they will already have left to return to Africa.

Swifts can catch up to 10,000 insects a day.

Swift

The swift visits every summer. It is dark brown with long, curved wings and a short, forked tail. Swifts fly high and are some of the fastest fliers in the bird world. They are always flying and feed, mate and even sleep in the air!

swift

🕊 16–17 cm

🌦 summer

🔭 common

🏠 towns, lakes

🗣 harsh, screaming screech

🍃 flying insects

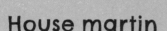

house martin

🐦 12.5 cm

🐛 summer

👀 common

🏠 towns and villages

🔊 *priit* flight call, soft twittering song

🌿 flying insects

House martin

The house martin is a summer visitor. It has a blue-black back, a black, forked tail and is white underneath. A house martin has no red and doesn't have the long tail streamers a swallow does. They often build their nests under the eaves of houses and barns.

House martins spend the winter in Africa, but scientists still don't know very much about exactly where they go.

house martin

Sand martin

The sand martin is a summer visitor. It has a brown back and is white underneath. It nests in sandy cliffs. Sadly, fewer and fewer sand martins make it across the growing Sahara Desert each year.

Skylark

The skylark is a medium-sized songbird. It is pale brown and streaky with a brown crest on its head. It is found in farm fields, meadows and sand dunes. The skylark performs a remarkable song display in spring. It flies up high, hovers, then sails downwards, singing all the while.

skylark

🕊 18–19 cm

☀ year-round

🏠 farmland, grassland, moorland, coasts

🎵 *chirrup* call, warbling song

🍃 insects, spiders, slugs, snails, grain, leaves

meadow pipit

Rock pipit

The rock pipit is a small songbird. It is slightly larger, darker and greyer than a meadow pipit, and has dark legs. It is found on rocky coasts all year round. Look out for it picking insects and other tiny animals from seaweed.

The skylark's song display can last up to five minutes.

skylark

The skylark was once very well known as a bird of the countryside. It is rarer now. It nests on the ground so is in danger from animals that want to eat its eggs and chicks.

Meadow pipit

Birdwatchers often talk about 'little brown birds' and the meadow pipit is one! It is a small, pale brown-grey bird with a speckled belly and thin orange legs. If you're walking on moorland in summer, most of the little birds you see are likely to be meadow pipits.

meadow pipit

🐦 14.5 cm

🐛 year-round

🏠 moorland

🎵 thin whistling call, song is a run of high notes ending with a trill

🍃 flies, beetles, spiders, seeds

rock pipit

🐦 16.5–17 cm

🐛 year-round

🏠 rocky seaside

🎵 high-pitched *peep*, warbling song

🍃 flies, midges, beetles, snails

Pied wagtail

The pied wagtail is a small black, white and grey bird. The
male has a black back and the female's is grey. Pied wagtails
often live near water, but can be seen in lots of other places
too, such as roofs, lawns, car parks and playing fields. Look
for one wagging its tail up and down as it walks along, or
busily flying here and there chasing flies and other insects.

*At night, pied wagtails roost
huddled up in groups, sometimes
thousands of birds together.*

pied wagtail

🐦 18 cm

🐛 year-round

🏠 countryside and towns

🎵 sharp *chizik* flight call, twittering song

🍃 flies, caterpillars, other insects

pied wagtail (female)

'Pied' is an old word meaning black and white.

pied wagtail (male)

Yellow wagtail

The yellow wagtail is nearly all yellow, with a greenish-yellow back, yellow underneath and yellow face. It has black legs. It is a summer visitor found on farms, especially near cows and horses.

All wagtails have a distinctive bounding flight.

grey wagtail

🐦 18–19 cm

🕷 year-round

🏠 streams, rivers, ponds, canals

🗣 sharp *tswik* flight call

🐛 insects, spiders, small water snails, tadpoles

Grey wagtail

The grey wagtail is grey and yellow. It has a grey back, face and tail, it is bright yellow under its tail and has pale legs. The male has a black throat in summer. Look out for a grey wagtail beside water, wagging its long tail up and down.

grey wagtail
(male)

grey wagtail
(female)

The grey wagtail's tail is very long – longer than a pied wagtail's.

Dipper

The dipper is a plump bird that looks like a big wren. It is black-brown with a white bib. It lives near fast-flowing rivers and streams in hilly areas. It bobs up and down on a rock, and dips into the water to catch insects, tadpoles and worms. It walks underwater too — it is the only bird in the UK that can do this.

The dipper has a third eyelid that protects its eyes when it dives, swims or walks underwater.

dipper

18 cm

year-round

fast-flowing rivers and streams in hilly areas

sharp *zit zit* flight call, warbling song

water insects, tadpoles, worms

A special membrane keeps its nostrils closed underwater.

dipper

Stonechat

The stonechat is a noisy little bird found on moors and heaths. The male has a black head, white neck patch and red-brown chest, and the female is paler. Its call sounds like stones being struck together.

The wheatear's name comes from old words for 'white' and 'rump'.

Wheatear

The wheatear is a summer visitor found in moorland. It has a grey back and head, black 'mask' across its eyes, black wings and a white rump. In flight it shows a black T-bar on its tail.

Redstart

The redstart is a summer visitor. The male has a grey head, back and throat, and is reddish underneath with a reddish tail. It flicks its tail up and down all the time. The female is brownish with a reddish tail.

'Start' is an old word for 'tail'.

Nightingale

The nightingale is a small brown bird, like a robin but without the red breast. It is so secretive though that you are unlikely to see it. It is known instead for its beautiful song, heard after dusk or before dawn in spring.

Dunnock

The dunnock is a small brown-and-grey bird. It has a thin black beak. It creeps around in bushes looking for insects and worms to eat. An old name for it is hedge sparrow.

All of the birds on this spread are about the same size as a robin.

Robin

The robin is a little brown bird with a bright orange-red breast. Look out for it in gardens and parks, bobbing its head up and down and searching for worms, seeds and fruit. Robins sing all year round to keep other robins away from their territory, and they also use their bright breast as a danger signal to warn other robins to stay away.

robin

🐦 14 cm

🐜 year-round

👓 common

🏠 almost every habitat

🔊 *tic tic* call, sweet song all year round

🌿 spiders, beetles, flies, worms, berries, grain

The robin is one of the few songbirds that sing in winter.

robin

In winter, robins puff up their feathers to keep warm.

Robins are often very tame and will follow gardeners to see what they are doing — especially if they have disturbed any worms for a robin to catch.

Wrens are our most common breeding bird with more than 8.5 million breeding pairs.

wren

Wren

The wren is a tiny brown bird with a big voice. It has a pale stripe above its eye, and its tail sticks up. It lives in just about every habitat. It has a loud song and sometimes its whole body shakes when it sings. On winter nights wrens flock together in communal roosts — with more than 60 snuggling up together to keep warm!

wren

🐦 9 –10 cm

🐝 year-round

🔭 common

🏠 almost every habitat

🔊 sharp *tik tik* call, loud, rattling song

🍃 insects, other invertebrates

A wren weighs less than a pencil.

blackbird
(female)

Blackbirds sometimes make a clucking noise when alarmed.

Blackbird

The blackbird is a smallish bird with a bright orange beak and yellow rings around its eyes. This is the male — only the male blackbird lives up to its name, while the female is brown and the young are brown and spotty. Blackbirds especially like living in gardens. Look out for one tilting its head towards the ground, looking for the movements of worms in the soil below. It attracts worms to the surface by stamping its feet. Listen for its loud, musical song.

blackbird

🐦 24–25 cm

🐝 year-round

👀 common

🏠 woodland, parks, gardens

💬 shrill *chink chink chink* call and rich song

🌿 insects, worms, berries

Baby blackbirds leave the nest before they can actually fly, and hop and scramble around until they learn to fly.

blackbird
(male)

Mistle thrush

The mistle thrush is a large thrush, slightly bigger than a blackbird. It is brown above and has a spotty chest and a dark beak. It sings from high in a tall tree, even in stormy weather. It will defend its food fiercely — it's even brave enough to chase away crows.

mistle thrush

mistle thrush

🐦 27 cm

🦗 year-round

🔭 common

🏠 woodland, parkland

🗣 loud, rattling call, loud song

🍃 insects, worms, slugs, snails, berries, fruit

The mistle thrush gets its name because it eats mistletoe—and it poos out the berries, spreading the plant's seeds.

Song thrush

The song thrush is slightly smaller than a blackbird. It has a spotty chest and a lovely, musical song. Song thrushes are experts at eating snails. They break the shells open by smashing them on stones. In winter, when there are not so many snails about, they like to eat berries.

When it flies you can see a yellow-brown patch under its wing.

song thrush

song thrush

🐦 23 cm

🦗 year-round

🔭 common

🏠 woodland, parks, gardens

🗣 thin *tsic* call, loud, tuneful song

🍃 snails, worms, insects, berries

Fieldfare

The fieldfare is a medium-sized thrush, slightly larger than a blackbird. It looks like a song thrush or mistle thrush, but has darker wings, a grey head and a yellowish throat and beak. It is a winter visitor. Look out for noisy flocks of fieldfares, often with redwings and other thrushes, when the weather is cold. Often they will eat all the berries in one place, then move on.

Fieldfares breed in Scandinavia.

fieldfare

fieldfare

🐦 25.5 cm

🦋 winter visitor

🔭 common

🏠 fields, parks, hedgerows, orchards

🔊 chattering *chak chack-chak* flight call

🌿 insects, worms, berries

Redwing

The redwing is our smallest thrush. It gets its name from the red patch under its wing, which is very obvious when it flies. It has a white stripe over its eye, and is brown above and spotted underneath. Look out for flocks of redwings in bushes or on the ground, feeding on berries or fallen fruit.

redwing

All of these thrushes like to eat fallen apples in winter. You can put some out on the ground to attract them to your garden.

redwing

🐦 21 cm

🦋 winter visitor

🔭 common

🏠 farmland, parks, hedgerows, orchards

🔊 soft *seep* flight call

🌿 berries, insects, worms, slugs, snails

Surprising visitors

Waxwing

The waxwing is a smallish, pinkish-brown bird with colourful black, yellow and white markings. It has small bright red patches on its wings that look like drops of wax. It is a rare winter visitor that loves to eat berries.

Hoopoe

The hoopoe is a bright orange-pink bird with black and white wings and tail and an elaborate crest on its head. It is a rare spring visitor. Its name comes from its call, which sounds like 'hoop, hoop, hoop'.

Golden oriole

The golden oriole is a colourful bird the size of a blackbird. The male is bright yellow and black, and the female is pale green and black with bright yellow patches. It is a very rare spring visitor and despite its bright colours it is good at hiding in trees.

Ring-necked parakeets are originally from Asia and Africa. In this country they escaped from captivity more than 40 years ago and now more than 30,000 live in the wild, and cope very well with our cold winters.

Ring-necked parakeet

The ring-necked parakeet is a medium-sized parrot. It looks very exotic — bright green with a red bill and a pink and black ring around its neck, with a very long tail. These parrots form large flocks and can be very noisy with their screeching call. They feed on buds, fruit and nuts.

sedge
warbler

*The sedge warbler
is a creamier colour
than the reed warbler.*

*The male stops
singing once a
female arrives.*

sedge warbler

🐦 13 cm

🐝 summer visitor

🏠 reed beds, ditches

🎵 *chirr chirr* call, long,
chattering song

🍃 insects, spiders, worms,
snails

Sedge warbler

The sedge warbler is a little brown warbler. It has
a bold pale stripe over its eye and a streaky back.
It is a summer visitor and nests in thick vegetation,
usually near water. As with all songbirds, a male
sedge warbler sings to attract a female. No
two songs are ever the same.

*Warblers are a
group of small
songbirds. To
warble means
to sing.*

Reed warblers are good at hiding, even when they're singing.

reed warbler

Reed warbler

The reed warbler is a little brown warbler, with just a very faint pale stripe over its eye. It is a summer visitor. It nests in reed beds by weaving a cup-shaped nest in the reeds, which it makes extra deep so that the chicks won't be blown away if it's windy.

reed warbler

🕊 13 cm

🐛 summer visitor

🏠 reed beds, marshes, ditches

🎵 sharp *chrrr* alarm call, long, chattering song

🌿 insects, spiders, snails

Cuckoos often lay their eggs in reed warblers' nests.

Blackcap

The blackcap is a small warbler the size of
a great tit. The male has a black cap and the
female has a brown cap. It is a common summer
visitor to woods, and some blackcaps stay all
year. In winter they like to eat mistletoe
and other berries.

blackcap
(male)

blackcap

🐦 13 cm

🐛 summer visitor but some
stay all year round

🏠 woodland, parks, gardens

🗣 harsh *tac* and
cherrr calls, tuneful song

🌿 insects, berries

whitethroat

Whitethroat

The whitethroat is a small warbler, the size
of a great tit. It gets its name from its white
throat. The male has a grey head and the
female has a brown head. It is a summer
visitor that mostly hides in bushes but will
often pop out on top of a bush.

whitethroat

🐦 14 cm

🐛 summer visitor

🏠 hedgerows, moorland

🗣 *tac tac* and *cherr* calls,
scratchy song

🌿 insects, berries

Chiffchaff

The chiffchaff is a small warbler, the size of a blue tit. It is greenish-brown above and pale below, with a pale stripe over its eye and dark legs. It is a summer visitor found in woods and bushes. It gets its name from its repetitive 'chiff-chaff' song. It flits from branch to branch, flicking its wings and tail, and it sometimes catches insects as it flies.

Many warblers look very similar and are hard to tell apart. Sometimes it's just the song that is the giveaway.

chiffchaff

chiffchaff

🐦 10–11 cm

🐛 summer visitor

👀 common

🏠 woodland, parks, gardens

🎵 *chiff-chaff* song

🌿 insects

Goldcrest

The goldcrest is not a warbler but it too is tiny — it is Europe's smallest bird. It has a bright yellow, orange and black crest on the top of its head, and a large black eye. It has a pale, greenish back and is cream underneath. It is found in woods, especially pine woods. Look out for it hanging upside down on pine branches to pick insects from underneath the needles.

goldcrest

🐦 9 cm

🐛 year-round

👀 common

🏠 woodland, parks, gardens

🎵 high-pitched *seee* call, *tseedle-dee tseedle-dee* song

🌿 insects, spiders

goldcrest (male)

spotted
flycatcher
(female)

*Flycatchers are
summer visitors.*

Spotted
flycatcher

The spotted flycatcher is
a little acrobat in flight. It
darts from a perch to catch
flying insects, twisting and
turning in the air, and then
returns to the same perch. It
is greyish-brown above and
pale below, with streaky
spots on its breast and
head. It lives in woods.

spotted flycatcher

🐦 14.5 cm

🌤 summer visitor

🏠 woods, parks, gardens

🎵 thin *zeee* call, soft,
warbly song

🌿 insects

pied flycatcher

🐦 13 cm

🪲 summer visitor

🏠 woods

🗨️ sharp *huit* call

🍃 insects

pied
flycatcher
(male)

Pied flycatcher

The pied flycatcher is smaller and
plumper than the spotted flycatcher.
The male is black and white and the
female is grey-brown and white.
It flutters and hovers in the air to
catch flying insects, and feeds
on the ground too.

Blue tit

The lively, noisy blue tit is one of our best-known garden birds. It has a yellow breast, white cheeks and a bright blue cap. Blue tits will happily use nest boxes and a pair of blue tits can catch hundreds of caterpillars a day to feed to their chicks. Look out for blue tits hanging upside down on your bird feeder or darting about from bush to bush.

blue tit

🐦 11.5 cm

🐛 year-round

👀 common

🏠 gardens, parks, woods

💬 thin *see* call and churring alarm call

🍃 insects, caterpillars, spiders, berries, nuts, seeds

By the time blue tit chicks leave the nest, they may have eaten up to 10,000 caterpillars.

blue tit

A female blue tit produces more than her own weight in eggs – 7 to 14 in a clutch. She lays them over several days.

Look out for a group of babies lined up in a tree waiting to be fed.

long-tailed tit

Long-tailed tit

This tiny acrobatic bird lives up to its name, as its tail is twice as long as its body! The long-tailed tit has a black and pink back, a black-and-white striped head and is pale pink underneath. In winter, small flocks of around 20 birds roost cuddled up together to keep warm.

long-tailed tit

🐦 14 cm

🌧 year-round

🔭 common

🏠 gardens, parks, woods

🗣 high-pitched *see see* call, with short, hissing trills

🍃 insects and their eggs and larvae, seeds

Coal tit

The coal tit is the smallest member of the tit family. You can recognise it from the thick white stripe on the back of its coal-black head. Coal tits like to live in conifer woods, and their thin bills are great for poking amongst long conifer needles and cones. They also visit garden bird feeders.

coal tit

🐦 11.5 cm

🐝 year-round

👀 common

🏠 gardens, parks, woods

💬 thin *see see* call, loud *pee-chew, pee-chew* song

🍃 insects, caterpillars, spiders

In snowy weather, coal tits feed on insects living underneath tree bark.

coal tit

Marsh tit

The marsh tit has a glossy black cap. It doesn't have a pale patch on its head or wings like a coal tit does. It sometimes joins groups of other tits in gardens.

Coal and marsh tits hide seeds to save for a rainy day. The part of their brain that deals with remembering things is big for their size.

great tit

🐦 14 cm

🐛 year-round

🔭 common

🏠 gardens, parks, woods

🗣 lots of different songs, all with a two-note pattern, including *tea-cher, tea-cher*

🌿 insects, caterpillars, seeds, nuts

A great tit uses its powerful bill to open nuts and seeds.

great tit

Great tit

The great tit is the largest member of the tit family. It is a favourite garden bird. It has a black head, white cheeks, green back and a yellow breast with a black stripe down the middle. It eats a wide variety of food and it sometimes bullies the smaller tits to make sure it gets the best food.

Willow tit

The willow tit is so similar to the marsh tit that the best way to tell them apart is to learn their songs. But its black cap is larger than a marsh tit's, and is dull rather than glossy, and it has a pale pattern on its wings. It lives in damp woodland areas.

A nuthatch sticks mud all around its nest hole to make the entrance just the right size, and to keep other birds out.

nuthatch

nuthatch

🐦 14 cm

🐛 year-round

👀 common

🏠 woods, parks, gardens

🗣 loud *dueet-dueet*, also *pee-pee-pee-pee* trill

🌿 insects, spiders, nuts, seeds

Nuthatches are the only birds that can walk down a tree trunk. But they walk up them too!

Nuthatch

The nuthatch is a handsome, noisy little bird that looks a bit like a small woodpecker. It has a blue-grey back, a black eye stripe and is orange underneath. Look out for it walking upside down on a tree trunk. It taps loudly on the bark, hammering nuts and digging out insects with its strong, pointed beak.

Treecreeper

The treecreeper is a shy, quiet bird that creeps up tree trunks. It shuffles up the tree, going round and round in a spiral, then flies down to the bottom of another tree and starts again. It has a speckly brown back and a white eye stripe. It has a thin, down-curved beak, which it uses to pick insects out of the bark.

It sleeps in cracks in the tree bark.

treecreeper

A treecreeper has long claws to cling on to the tree bark.

treecreeper

🐦 12.5 cm

☀ year-round

🔭 common

🏠 woods

🗣 thin *tsee tsee* call, very high-pitched trilling sound

🍃 insects

Jay

The jay is a big, colourful crow. It has
a pink-brown body, a black moustache
and shiny blue and black wing patches.
Although jays are so colourful, they are
difficult to see because they are shy.
They fly off with a loud screech if
they're disturbed. Jays are famous
for burying acorns in autumn
to eat in winter.

*Look out for a
flash of white rump
when a jay flies.*

*Some of the acorns
that jays bury end up
growing into new trees.*

jay

*Its harsh call
frightens off other
woodland birds.*

	jay
🕊	34–35 cm
🐛	year-round
👓	common
🏠	woods, gardens
🗣	loud screech
🌿	acorns, other seeds, nuts, insects, other birds' eggs and young

Magpie

The magpie is a large crow. It is black and white, but its black wings and tail are iridescent and can look blue or green in the light. Magpies are noisy and chatter with each other as they go about looking for food. Listen for their loud, rattling call. They are found in towns and the countryside.

magpie

🕊 44–46 cm

🌦 year-round

👓 common

🏠 woods, farmland, towns, gardens, parks

🗣 loud rattling sound

🍃 fruit, berries, insects, worms, other birds' eggs and young, carrion (dead animals)

Magpies and other crows are known for eating other birds' eggs and chicks. But this is natural – the real problem for small birds is that there is not enough food or places for them to nest.

magpie

Magpie pairs usually stay together for life.

Magpies also store food when there is lots of it. They dig a hole in the ground with their beak, put the food in it and cover the hole with a stone or leaf.

Carrion crow

The carrion crow is a big, all-black crow with a thick black beak. It gets its name because it eats carrion (dead animals), but it will eat almost anything. These crows live almost anywhere and are usually seen alone or in pairs. They are very clever. For example, they will smash seashells open by flying up and dropping them on rocks.

Members of the crow family are some of the most intelligent animals of all. In an experiment, a carrion crow worked out an eight-step puzzle to get at some food.

carrion crow

carrion crow

- 45–47 cm
- year-round
- common
- farmland, woods, parks, gardens, towns and cities
- deep, cawing *kraaa kraaa*
- carrion, young birds and mammals, eggs, insects, worms, grain, seeds, fruit, shellfish

Rook

The rook looks a lot like a carrion crow but it is slightly smaller, with a patch of bare grey skin around its beak. It also has baggy feather 'trousers'. Rooks gather in big flocks, usually on farmland. They nest in rookeries, which are big groups of nests in the tops of trees.

rook

rook

- 44–46 cm
- year-round
- common
- farmland, woods
- grating croaks
- worms, grain, nuts, beetles, caterpillars, birds, eggs, carrion

Jackdaw

The jackdaw is a small black crow with a silvery head. Look out for its pale eyes and the way it stands upright. Jackdaws are noisy and are often seen in fields or parks with rooks. They have a shorter bill than other crows.

Jackdaws communicate using a complicated system of different poses and calls.

jackdaw

- 🕊 33–34 cm
- 🌦 year-round
- 🔭 common
- 🏠 farmland, woods, towns
- 💬 sharp *jack jack* and higher-pitched *kyow*
- 🌿 insects, grain, seeds, fruit, berries, eggs, young birds, rubbish

jackdaw

raven

- 🕊 64 cm
- 🌦 year-round
- 🏠 cliffs, mountains, moors
- 💬 deep, *kronk kronk* croak
- 🌿 carrion, mammals, birds, eggs, insects

Raven

The raven is the biggest crow in the world. It is all black with long wings and a huge, powerful beak. Look out for its diamond-shaped tail. Ravens usually nest on cliffs. They make a deep 'croak, croak' noise. They are acrobatic flyers and can even fly upside down.

Sometimes peregrine falcons will take over an old raven nest.

raven

Starling

The starling looks black but in fact its feathers are shiny purple and green, with lots of white spots in winter. Look out for starlings waddling along the ground or loudly quarrelling over food. They gather in enormous groups at dusk to roost — sometimes more than a million flock together!

starling

🐦 21.5 cm

🐛 year-round

🔭 common

🏠 gardens, parks, farmland, towns and cities, rubbish tips, beaches

🗣 complicated song with rattles and whistles, copies other birds' calls

🌿 insects and their larvae, worms, spiders, berries, fruit

Look for its pointed beak and short tail.

starling

Starlings can copy the songs of other birds or even ringtones and car alarms!

House sparrow numbers are falling, and scientists are studying why this might be.

house sparrow (female)

House sparrows can nest from April to August and rarely all year round. They don't mind nesting really close together.

House sparrow

The house sparrow is one of our commonest birds. The male has a grey cap, black bib and brown-and-black feathers on its back. The female is plainer. House sparrows like to live near people. Watch them fighting and chasing each other, chirping noisily all the while.

house sparrow (male)

house sparrow

- 14–15 cm
- year-round
- common
- towns and cities, gardens, parks, farmland
- chirps and chirrups
- seeds, scraps, greenflies, caterpillars

Chaffinch

The chaffinch is a small, brightly coloured bird. The male is pink with a blue-grey cap, chestnut back and black-and-white wings with a green patch. The female is a paler pinkish-brown and doesn't have the blue-grey cap. Chaffinches often pick up seeds that other birds have spilled from bird feeders.

A chaffinch's song is different from one part of the country to another.

chaffinch (female)

Although it's colourful, its patterned plumage helps the chaffinch to blend in when it's feeding on the ground.

chaffinch (male)

chaffinch

🐦 14.5 cm

☀️ year-round

🔭 common

🏠 gardens, parks, woods, farmland

📢 loud *chink-chink* call and rattling song

🌿 seeds, insects, caterpillars

Greenfinch

The greenfinch is a plump finch with a thick head and beak. The male is mostly green, with bright yellow patches on its wings and tail. The female is browner with the same bright yellow patches. Greenfinches especially love to eat peanuts and sunflower seeds. They use their thick beaks to crack them open.

greenfinch

- 🐦 15 cm
- 🐛 year-round
- 🔍 common
- 🏠 gardens, parks, woods, farmland
- 🗨 loud twittering trill followed by long *dzeeeeeee*
- 🍃 seeds

greenfinch
(male)

greenfinch
(female)

Look out for the yellow wing and tail flashes and forked tail when it flies.

Linnet

The linnet is a lively finch that chatters and twitters. The male has a grey head and a rose-red spot on its forehead and breast. Linnets live on farmland and moorland and are becoming rarer.

Bullfinch

The bullfinch is a large, colourful finch. The male is mainly bright pink, while the female is a paler brownish-pink. Both have a black cap and a grey back. Bullfinches are shy birds. They use their thick, strong bills to eat buds and seeds.

Yellowhammer

The yellowhammer is a bunting that lives on farmland. The male has a yellow head, streaky brown back and streaky yellow chest. He will often sing from the tops of bushes or hedges.

Redpoll

The redpoll gets its name from its red cap – 'poll' is an old word for head. It has a streaky back and paler streaky belly. It is a winter visitor and likes to live where there are birch trees.

Reed bunting

The reed bunting lives in reed beds and other wet places. The male has a black head and bib, brown streaky back and white collar. Reed buntings flock together with finches and pipits in winter.

Crossbill

This large finch gets its name from its unusual beak, which has one part crossing over the other. This makes a great tool for pulling seeds out of pine cones. The male crossbill is red and the female is grey-green.

Goldfinch

The goldfinch is a small, very colourful finch. It has a red, white and black face and a yellow band on its wings. Look out for a yellow flash when it flies. Goldfinches love to eat thistle seeds and you may see several birds perched on a clump of thistles, picking out the seeds with their pointed beaks. They also visit gardens. Look for their dancing flight and listen for their tinkling calls.

goldfinch

Goldfinches sometimes decorate their nests with flowers.

goldfinch

🐦 12 cm

☀ year-round

🔭 common

🏠 gardens, farmland, waste ground

🎵 simple *twit-a-twit* flight call, long, twittering song

🍃 mainly seeds, also insects

Siskin

The siskin looks a bit like a greenfinch, with a green back and yellow and black wings, but it is smaller, with a yellow face and streaky belly. The male has a black cap. It sometimes visits garden bird feeders and will hang upside down. It can hang on to very thin twigs to reach food.

Siskins can be seen all year round but many more come here in winter.

siskin

🕊 12 cm

🐛 year-round

🏠 woods, parks, gardens

🗣 *tzeuu* or *tzuee* call, twittering song

🌿 mainly seeds, also insects

siskin (male)

GETTING INVOLVED WITH BIRDS

In the garden

One way to get involved with birds is to encourage them to visit your garden or any outdoor space you have. To create a good habitat for birds you need to make sure they have food, water, places to shelter and somewhere to nest.

Food

You can put out food on a bird table and in hanging bird feeders in trees or bushes. There are even feeders you can stick to a window. A bird table needs to be out in the open, not near anywhere cats might hide.

You can also attract birds by growing plants that appeal to insects they like to feed on, or that have seeds that birds like to eat. Ask if you can plant some sunflowers or poppies, and leave a patch of weeds — such as nettles and thistles — somewhere in the garden.

Bird favourites

poppy seeds, rose hips, honeysuckle berries, sunflower seeds, scabious, ivy berries, teasel seeds, hawthorn berries, holly berries, silver birch seeds, rowan berries, elderberry fruits

Nests

Trees, bushes, hedges and even sheds make good places for birds to nest. You can also put up a nest box. There are different sizes for different birds, but the most common kind is great for blue tits.

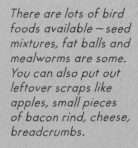

There are lots of bird foods available — seed mixtures, fat balls and mealworms are some. You can also put out leftover scraps like apples, small pieces of bacon rind, cheese, breadcrumbs.

Joining in

Another way to get involved with birds is to
join in with others to get out and about. There
are lots of clubs you can join to share your
interest in birds with other people. RSPB Wildlife
Explorers is the junior part of the RSPB: being a
member allows you to take part in competitions,
events and projects, and you get six magazines
a year. Perhaps your school or local area has
a bird club or nature or conservation club.
You could even start your own!

Conservation
*Taking part in wildlife conservation is a great way to
get involved with birds! Your local RSPB reserve may
offer activities such as planting trees, building bug
hotels or putting up nest boxes.*

Water
*A bird bath gives birds
clean water to drink and
somewhere to wash
their feathers.*

*In very cold weather,
put out food and
water twice a day.
Keep feeders, bird
tables and bird
baths clean, to avoid
spreading disease.
Read more about
preventing disease at
www.rspb.org.uk*

*It's OK to feed birds all
year round, but they
need less from you
in summer and fatty
foods may go off.*

CREATING YOUR OWN BIRD RECORD

It can be fun and interesting to record the birds you see. All you need is a notebook and pencil. In your notebook, write down where you saw the bird, the date and time, what the weather was like, what the bird was doing, and anything else that seems interesting. If you can, make a sketch or take a photograph. You don't need to be a brilliant artist — even a rough drawing will help you remember what you saw.

Instead of a notebook, you can just tick off the birds you see on a checklist — like the one at the back of this book!

Bird: Blue Tit
Where: Gran's garden
Date: 2nd April
Weather: Sunny

Notes: Blue tit was at the feeder, kept hanging upside down!

green bit on his wing

Bright yellow!

Binoculars

As you get more involved in birdwatching, you may want to use binoculars to see birds better. If you can, try out a few pairs in the shop and get advice on what to buy. It's important to get a pair that's light. RSPB shops can help you with this. Find your nearest one at shopping.rspb.org.uk

Cameras

Taking really good pictures of birds requires a lot of patience and skill, and sometimes a fancy camera with a powerful zoom! But you can have fun taking photographs with a mobile phone or a camera. You can even record birdsong on your phone.

Bird: Robin
Where: The park
Date: 15th April
Weather: Cloudy

Notes: Robin was sitting on the park fence and ran under bushes.

orange/
Red

grey bit

CLUBS TO DISCOVER

You can find out about these organisations and their projects and activities:

RSPB Wildlife Explorers
www.rspb.org.uk/youth

British Trust for Ornithology (BTO)
www.bto.org

Wildfowl and Wetlands Trust
www.wwt.org.uk

*The Wildlife Trusts
(and Wildlife Watch)*
www.wildlifetrusts.org

Birding For All
www.birdingforall.com

Activities to try

Why not try these fun
bird-related activities?

Make a bird cake

You will need:

- *good quality bird seed*
- *raisins*
- *grated cheese*
- *suet or lard*
- *yoghurt pots*
- *string*
- *mixing bowl*
- *scissors*

1. Carefully make a small hole in the bottom
of a yoghurt pot. Thread string through the
hole and tie a knot on the inside. Leave enough
string so that you can tie the pot to a tree
or to your bird table.

2. Allow the lard to warm up to room
temperature, but don't melt it. Then cut it up
into small pieces and put it in the mixing bowl.

3. Add the other ingredients to the bowl and mix
them together with your fingertips. Keep adding
the seed/raisin/cheese mixture and squidging it
until the fat holds it all together.

*Don't put the cake
where dogs might
be able to get
the raisins.*

4. Fill your yoghurt pot with bird cake mixture
and put it in the fridge to set for an hour or so.

5. Hang your bird cakes from trees or your bird
table, and watch for birds!

Put up a nest box

You can buy a nest box from the RSPB or other good suppliers, or even make your own (there is a guide on the RSPB website). Then fix it at least two metres high on a tree or wall, facing somewhere between north and east to protect it from bad weather. Make sure there is a clear path to the nest box and the entrance is not hidden by any clutter. It's best to put your nest box up in autumn or winter. It's exciting if you get birds moving in to your nest box, but then you must leave them alone — don't peep inside.

Share your findings

Your bird spotting notes can be useful to birdwatchers and scientists studying bird numbers and behaviour.

You can also send your bird records to BirdTrack: www.birdtrack.net. (You need to register for this website, so make sure you get your parents' or guardian's permission and help for this.)

Find out more

Books

The RSPB Handbook of British Birds by Peter Holden and Tim Cleeves (Bloomsbury, 2014) — for more detail and more birds!

i-SPY Birds (Collins, 2016) — tick off the birds you spot and earn points depending how rare they are.

RSPB Birds: Explore their extraordinary world by Miranda Krestovnikoff and Angela Harding (Bloomsbury, 2020) — for amazing information about birds all over the world

Eyewitness Explorer: Nature Ranger by Richard Walker (Dorling Kindersley, 2015) - activities you can do out and about in nature

Websites and apps

www.rspb.org.uk

www.birdingforall.com

www.birdlife.org/worldwide/news/kids-birding

Birdtrack by BTO — app available from the App store or Google Play

Chirp! Bird Songs UK & Europe — app available from the App store

Places to go

The RSPB is the UK's largest nature conservation charity — it looks after birds and other wildlife and the environment. The RSPB has 180 nature reserves around the country. There is a huge variety of different places and different birds to see.

Top ten RSPB reserves for families:

Conwy
Dearne Valley Old Moor
Fairburn Ings
Loch Leven
Minsmere
Newport Wetlands
Pulborough Brooks
Radipole Lake
Rainham Marshes
Saltholme

More to explore

In the UK there are hundreds more nature reserves as well as the RSPB reserves. The Wildfowl and Wetlands Trust (WWT), National Trust and Scottish Wildlife Trust are just three of many organisations who have reserves you can visit, and there are many more local conservation trusts too. Your local park, river or lake, beach or woodland can also be a brilliant place to go birdwatching.

GLOSSARY

acorn the nut of an oak tree

bill another word for beak, the hard nose and mouthparts of a bird

breeding having babies. A breeding pair of birds is a male and female bird that get together to lay eggs and raise young

camouflage shape, colour or pattern that helps something hide

carrion dead animals

chick baby bird

colony a very large number of the same type of creature all living together

communal to do with a big group or community doing something together

conifer a kind of tree that has hard, scaly fruits called cones

conservation saving and looking after the environment and wildlife

courtship the way birds behave when they are trying to attract a mate

crest feathers sticking up on top of a bird's head

drought a long time when there is no rain

environment everything around us. It is made up of the air, ground, soil, and all living and non-living things

estuary flat, muddy area where a river meets the sea

extinction dying out altogether

filtering removing tiny things from water, a bit like using a sieve

flank another word for a bird's side

flock a big group of birds

habitat the type of place where a particular creature lives

hover fly almost on the spot, not moving forwards or backwards

invertebrate one of a huge group of animals that includes insects, spiders, worms, slugs, snails and many more

moorland a type of habitat with heather, rocky and boggy ground and very few trees

moulting losing old, worn feathers ready to grow new ones

nature reserve a place where nature and wildlife are specially protected

prey an animal that is eaten by other animals

iridescent shiny bright colours that seem to change depending on the light

larvae young insects. Caterpillars and grubs are some other names for larvae

mate a bird's mate is the partner it has babies with. To mate means to come together to make babies.

membrane a thin, skin-like layer of the body

migration moving every year from one part of the world to another, usually to find a good feeding place or somewhere to breed

remote far away from other things, or difficult to get to

roost the word for when a bird rests or sleeps. A roost is a place where lots of birds gather together to sleep

navigator someone or something that works out where to go

plumage another word for a bird's feathers or its overall colours and markings

predator an animal that hunts and eats other animals

talons the sharp, hooked claws of birds of prey

territory the place a bird thinks of as its own and defends against others

wattle a piece of bright, fleshy skin on a bird's face

BIRD CHECKLIST